What is Peace?

Images and words of
peace
by the students of

Academic Year 2014-2015

6015 Chillum Place, NE
Washington, DC 20011
www.shiningstarspcs.org

This book, *What Is Peace?* is published by Street to Street
Epic Publications, Washington, DC, under the direction of Dr. Carolivia Herron.

Text copyright © 2015 by Shining Stars Montessori Academy Public Charter School of
Washington, DC and the individual student artists.
Cover designed by Carolivia Herron
Cover graphic by Zoe W, student at Shining Stars Montessori Academy
Copyright graphic by Nico J

See carolivia.com
Published in the United States by Street to Street Epic Publica
www.carolivia.com
StreetToStreet.org
www.EpicCenterStories.org
www.ShiningStarsPCS.org

Library of Congress Cataloging-in-Publication Data
Shining Stars Montessori Academy Public Charter School of Washington, DC
What Is Peace?

Summary: Images and words of peace by primary and elementary school students of
Shining Stars Montessori Academy Public Charter School of Washington, DC, 2014-2015.
The students of five 2014-2015 classes: Angelou Stars, Bethune Stars, Gandhi Stars,
Montessori Stars, and Keller Stars, each creates a colorful page with words evoking
peace.

ISBN 978-1-938609-34-3

How does one begin to teach children about Peace?

How do we explain this concept to our young students? What is their understanding of this idea called "Peace"? How do we as adults teach children to recognize Peace and to live in peace in a global community wracked by war, poverty and hunger? How do we as a school teach and model the concepts of Peace today, for our students — who will be the 21st century leaders of tomorrow?

So how does one teach Peace to a child?

This question hangs heavily in my heart. How can we nurture and greenhouse a new generation **not** to think and behave like we have done? How do we teach them a new way?

Perhaps it is by helping them to create their own vision/image of Peace. To help them to create a clear image of what Peace is for them.

The 2015 Shining Stars Montessori Academy Public Charter School *Peace Project* asked our 3 to 10 year old students to create their own vision/images/poems of Peace. The Project is the first in a series of all-school social, economic, educational justice and equity themes and questions that we will be posing and working with our children throughout an entire school year, this year — and in years to come. We hope that you appreciate and enjoy their images and wisdom.

"Peace does not mean an absence of conflicts; differences will always be there. Peace means solving these differences through peaceful means; through dialogue, education, knowledge; and through humane ways." — Dalai Lama

Regina Rodriguez

Executive Director, Shining Stars Montessori Academy Public Charter School

Washington, DC, August 2015

Contents

Angelou Stars

"Try to be a rainbow in someone's cloud."

Maya Angelou

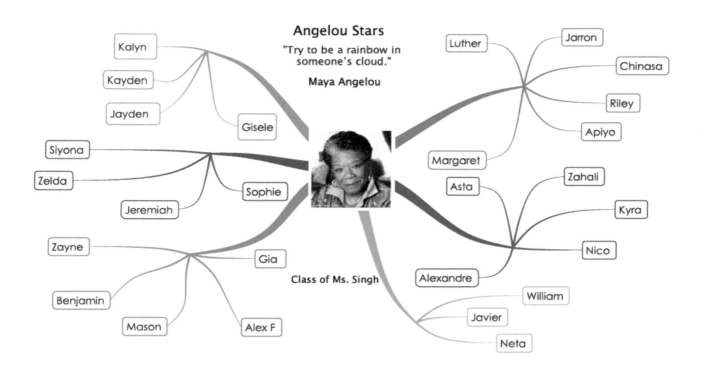

Kalyn

Kayden

Jayden

Gisele

Siyona

Zelda

Jeremiah

Sophie

Zayne

Gia

Benjamin

Mason

Alex F

Luther

Jarron

Chinasa

Riley

Apiyo

Margaret

Asta

Zahali

Kyra

Nico

Alexandre

William

Javier

Neta

Class of Ms. Singh

Luther

A Peaceful
Person

Luther

Chinasa

Peace by Chinasa

Apiyo

Apiyo
Peace

Asta

Asta

Peace is the colors.

Zahali

Zahali
Angelou Stone

Peace

Kyra

vuga

peace

Kyra

Nico

Peace

NICO

Alexandre

Angelou Stars   PEACE   Alexander

William

William   Peace place.

igelou   Stars

Javier

P
E
A
C
E

Neta
Angelou Stars

Gia

Alex F

Alex

Pence
RAINBOW

Mason

Peace

Mason
Angelou Stars

Benjamin

PeAce HANDS

Zayne

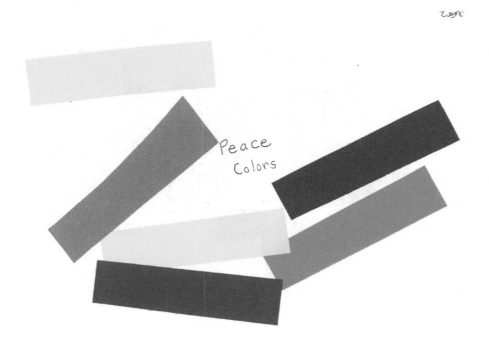

Peace
Colors

Zayn

Sophie

My brother is very funny and
that's why he makes me feel
peaceful when he makes me
giggle sometimes.

SOPHIE

Jeremiah

Jeremiah
Peace Project

Jeremiah is peaceful.

Zelda

peace

Zelda

Siyona

Siyona

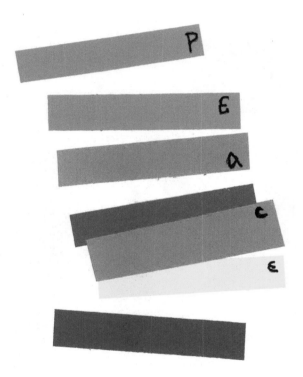

P
E
a
c
E

GISELE   I LIKE PEACE.

Jayden

Peace

Jayden

Jayden

Page 32

PEACE KAYDEN

Kalyn

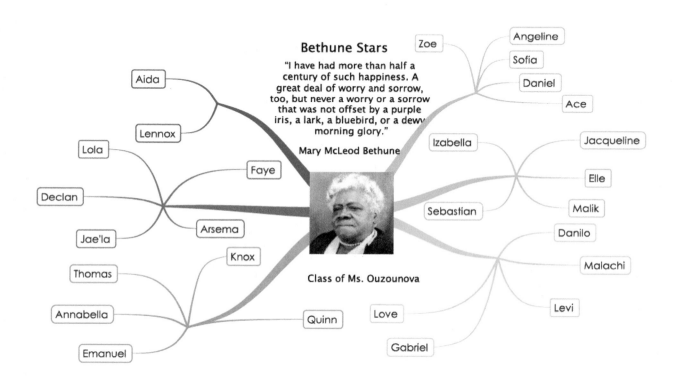

Bethune Stars

"I have had more than half a century of such happiness. A great deal of worry and sorrow, too, but never a worry or a sorrow that was not offset by a purple iris, a lark, a bluebird, or a dewy morning glory."

Mary McLeod Bethune

Class of Ms. Ouzounova

Aida
Lennox
Lola
Faye
Declan
Arsema
Jae'la
Knox
Thomas
Annabella
Emanuel
Quinn

Zoe
Angeline
Sofia
Daniel
Ace
Izabella
Jacqueline
Elle
Sebastian
Malik
Danilo
Malachi
Levi
Love
Gabriel

Zoe

Zoe

Peace is my family.

I love my family.

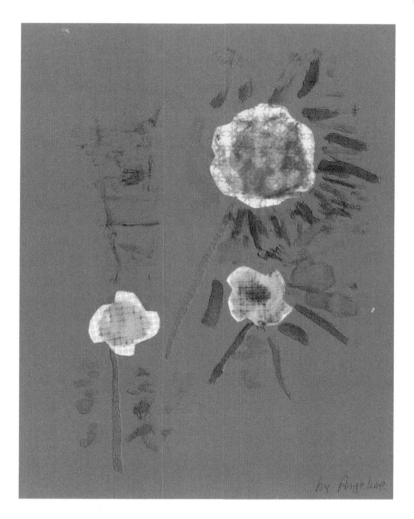

by Angeline

Sofia

Sofia

Peace is
Yellow hand
and
Pink flowers.

Page 38

Daniel

Most of the time
I feel peaceful
when I play with
my sisters.

Ace

is when
it is quiet

Jacqueline

Bethune

Page 42

by: Elle

Peace is my rainbow.

Malik

Sebastian

Peace is flowers -sebastian

Danilo

Danilo

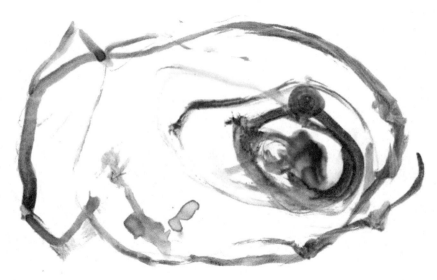

Peace is my purple fish.

MALACHi

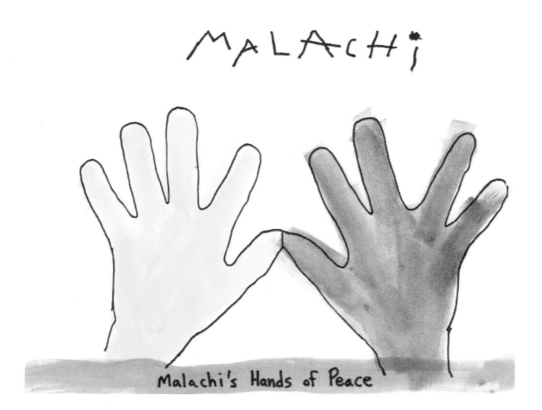

Malachi's Hands of Peace

Levi

Gabriel

Peace is
purple and green.

Love

Love

Peace is the
blue ocean.

Quinn

Peace is my home.   by Quinn

Emanuel

Annabella

Annabella

Thomas

peace   by: Thomas

by knox

Arsema

Jae'la

Jae'la

Peace is when Grandma and
my mommy feel good.

Declan

Peace, Mommy
and me, Declan.

Lola

Lola

Peace is working
with Ms. Sandy.

Bethune Stars

Faye

faye

Peace: my garden
and Mommy

Peace is the Zoo with lot's of animals.

Aida

Adia

Gandhi Stars

"If we want to reach real peace in this world, we should start by educating children."
Mohandas Gandhi

Caleb
Victoria
Atulegwu
Aalim
Kaylan
Stella W
Navaeh
Leontine
Rashid
Louis
Avery
Caden
Vernice

Gustavo
Solveig
Solle
Stella R
Freddie
Nikola
Nethanya
Dania
Sanaia
Clara
Tuli
Johanna
Nalani
Ivania
Elliot
Mateo F

Class of Ms. Pointdujour

Gustavo

Gustavo

I am
the driver
of the
Peace
Train.

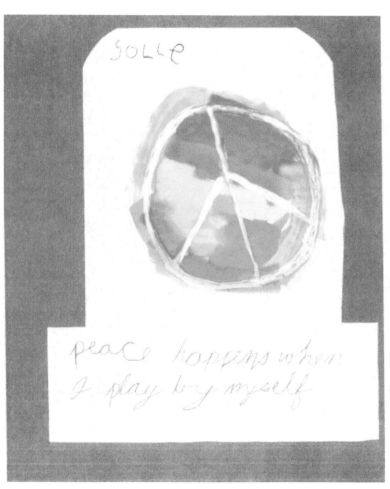

SOLLE

peace happens when
I play by myself

Stella R

Peace is when I eat dinner at the table.

Stella R.

PEACE

Freddie

Peace is being quiet when
I go to sleep.

Nikola

Nethanya

Dania

Peace means I feel safe and free.

SANAIA

Clara

CLARA

Gandhi
Stars

Tuli (Johanna)

Nalani

BRING PEACE

Elliot

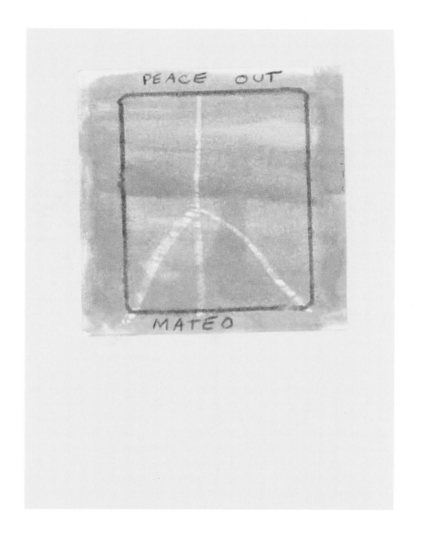

Vernice

Caden

CADEN

Avery

Rashid

RASHID

When I see birds
I feel peaceful.

Leontine

Peace

Leotine

Navaeh

Flowers and plants make me happy.

Neveah

Stella W

Kaylan

Kaylan

PEACE

Atulegwu

Atulegwu

Caleb

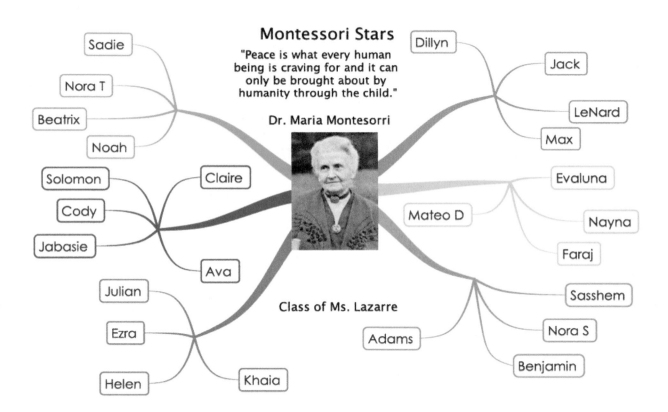

Montessori Stars

"Peace is what every human being is craving for and it can only be brought about by humanity through the child."

Dr. Maria Montesorri

Class of Ms. Lazarre

Sadie

Nora T

Beatrix

Noah

Solomon

Cody

Jabasie

Claire

Ava

Julian

Ezra

Helen

Khaia

Dillyn

Jack

LeNard

Max

Evaluna

Mateo D

Nayna

Faraj

Sasshem

Nora S

Adams

Benjamin

Dillyn

I feel peaceful when when I go

I feel peaceful when I am going to sleep, waking up, and playing with my new friends. ~ Jack Ralles

LeNard

I feel peaceful when at home
watching PAW PATROL

I feel peaceful when I hear birds sing, when I build with my blocks, and when I go to the playground.

MAX

Evaluna

I feel peaceful when

I feel peaceful when
I Doo Art+I feel peace
I feel peaceful when
I am HAPPY.

Faraj

I feel peaceful when I love my
family and they love me back.
Secret: I use my special weapon
My smile.

Faraj

Mateo
Delta

I feel peaceful when mami is tickling me, when I sleep whith papá, when I plag with Iota the dog at la finca.

Sasshem

I feel peaceful when I feel better

I feel peaceful when I walk in the forest, and when I go to the park.

Benjamin

Ben
Montessori Stars BO

I feel peaceful when I snuggle with
my Mom and Dad and when I fall
asleep.

I feel peaceful when I AM

outside

Adams

Khaia

Khaia

I feel peaceful when I say prayers
when I read a book and eat dinner.
It NAJA

Helen

Montessori Stars '05

I feel peaceful when

Helen

Page 105

Ezra

I feel peaceful when I'm at
Disneyland.

Ezra

Julian

I feel peaceful when at naptime
and when there is music
I like.

Ava

I feel peaceful when dressing up
in my Elsa dress.

Jabasie

Page 109

Cody

I feel peaceful when I hug my mom!

Page 110

I feel peaceful when I go to
the playground.

solomon

Claire

I feel peaceful when I am
painting.

Claire

Noah

I feel peaceful when
I'm nice

Noah

Beatrix

I feel peaceful when I'm picking
blueberries.

Beatrix

Page 114

I feel peaceful when I wake up on Saturday morning and when I'm reading.   —Nora Taty

Sadie

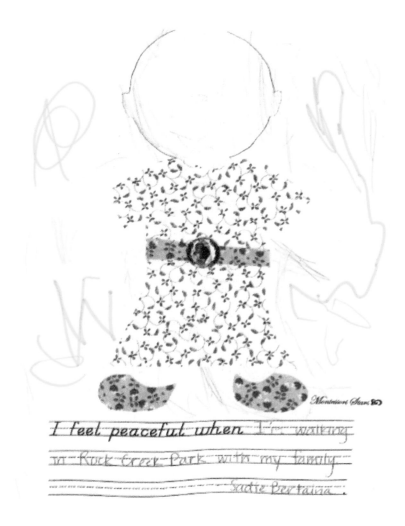

I feel peaceful when I'm walking
in Rock Creek Park with my family.
Sadie Bertaina.

Page 116

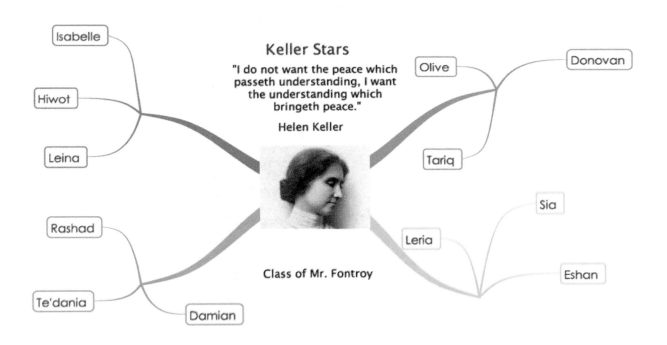

Keller Stars

"I do not want the peace which passeth understanding, I want the understanding which bringeth peace."

Helen Keller

Class of Mr. Fontroy

Isabelle

Hiwot

Leina

Rashad

Te'dania

Damian

Olive

Donovan

Tariq

Leria

Sia

Eshan

Olive

Donovan

Tariq

Sia

Eshan

PEACE ☮

UNSPOKEN nothing is heard   thoughts now deffered float in my mind
liked
   safe from all harm peacful and calm   settling within time to unwind and leave you

will find

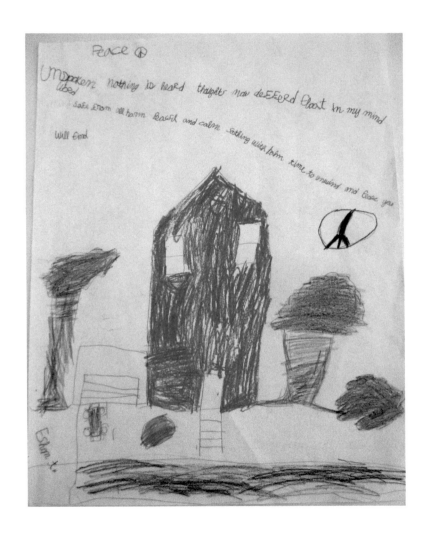

Eshan x

Page 123

Damian

Te'dania

Rashad

Leina

Nature is love.
Peace is love.
Peace is life.
Peace is friendship.
Mother Earth is peace.

Hiwot

Peace

I like peace.
Peace is when you are calm.
Peace is my family.
Peace is playing
with my friends.

About Shining Stars Montessori Academy Public Charter School

In 2008, a group of community activists, educators and parents sought to establish a new Montessori program to serve public school students in Washington, DC. In 2010, the District of Columbia Public Charter School Board approved the charter application and the vision of establishing Shining Stars Montessori Academy Public Charter School (SSMA) became a reality.

The SSMA founders chose the Montessori Method as its centering pedagogy because they were convinced that this approach can change the educational outcomes for children living in Washington, DC.

Located in Northeast Washington, DC, Shining Stars Montessori Academy is a small elementary school which has become enriched and reflective of the growing diversity of the nation's capital.

In 2014-2015, the school expanded to include four Primary level classes and one Lower Elementary class. They are Mary McLeod Bethune House (Bethune Stars), Maria Montessori House (Montessori Stars), Mohandas Gandhi House (Gandhi Stars), Helen Keller House (Keller Stars) and the newly created Dr. Maya Angelou House (Angelou Stars).

To continue Dr. Maria Montessori's work of "achieving world peace through education," SSMA launched its Peace Project 2015. Enjoy the artwork and thoughts of our children.

Acknowledgements

The Shining Stars Montessori Academy Public Charter Schools gives its thanks to all those who helped us complete this "What Is Peace?" publication project: Ms. Louise Parker Kelley, who collected the work of the students; the teachers, Ms. Singh, Ms. Ozuounova, Ms. Pointdujour, Ms. Lazarre, Mr. Fontroy, Ms. Tran, Mr. Vu, Mr. Zapata, Mr. Shepherd, Ms. Simpson, Ms. Thompson, Ms. Bush; Mr. Coleman, Mr. J. Williams, Ms. Mitchell, Ms. Rocker, Mr. C. Williams, Ms. Hall, Ms. Ivey, Mr. Guevara and other supporting staff and parents, as well as the executive oversight of Regina Rodriguez, Executive Director.

CPSIA information can be obtained
at www.ICGtesting.com
Printed in the USA
LVOW05s0100041017
551106LV00011B/727/P